T0390241

States of Matter
Volume

by Rebecca Pettiford

Bullfrog Books

Ideas for Parents and Teachers

Bullfrog Books let children practice reading informational text at the earliest reading levels. Repetition, familiar words, and photo labels support early readers.

Before Reading

- Discuss the cover photo. What does it tell them?

- Look at the picture glossary together. Read and discuss the words.

During Reading

- "Walk" through the book with the reader. Discuss new or unfamiliar words. Sound them out together.

- Look at the photos together. Point out the photo labels.

After Reading

- Prompt the child to think more. Ask: We can measure volume. One way is with measuring cups and spoons. Have you used measuring cups and spoons before? What did you measure?

Bullfrog Books are published by Jump!
5357 Penn Avenue South
Minneapolis, MN 55419
www.jumplibrary.com

Jump! is a division of FlutterBee Education Group.

Library of Congress Cataloging-in-Publication Data is available at www.loc.gov or upon request from the publisher.

ISBN: 979-8-89213-972-4 (hardcover)
ISBN: 979-8-89213-973-1 (paperback)
ISBN: 979-8-89213-974-8 (ebook)

Editor: Jenna Gleisner
Designer: Anna Peterson

Photo Credits: BELIMBINGperak/Shutterstock, cover; michelaubryphoto/Shutterstock, 1; ND700/Shutterstock, 3; Ilya_Starikov/iStock, 4 (foreground); KB Focused Imagery/Shutterstock, 4 (background), 8 (background), 19 (background), 20 (background); Ladanifer/Shutterstock, 5, 6–7, 23br; lucadp/Shutterstock, 8 (foreground), 20 (foreground); Teri Virbickis/Shutterstock, 8–9, 23tr; Crystal Madsen/Shutterstock, 10, 23bl; KrimKate/Shutterstock, 11; this_baker/Shutterstock, 12–13 (hand); Premyuda Yospim/iStock, 12–13 (bowl); Arina P Habich/Shutterstock, 14–15, 16–17; Photo Melon/Shutterstock, 18, 23tl; Mr.Rahim Mia/Shutterstock, 19 (left), 24; Daria Medvedeva/Shutterstock, 19 (right); Dan Kosmayer/Shutterstock, 20 (cookies); Prostock-Studio/iStock, 20–21; Leian/Shutterstock, 22 (top); Yellow Cat/Shutterstock, 22 (bottom).

Printed in the United States of America at Corporate Graphics in North Mankato, Minnesota.

Table of Contents

Fill It Up! 4

Measure Volume 22

Picture Glossary 23

Index 24

To Learn More 24

Fill It Up!

The flour jar is empty.

4

We fill it up!

flour ·····▶

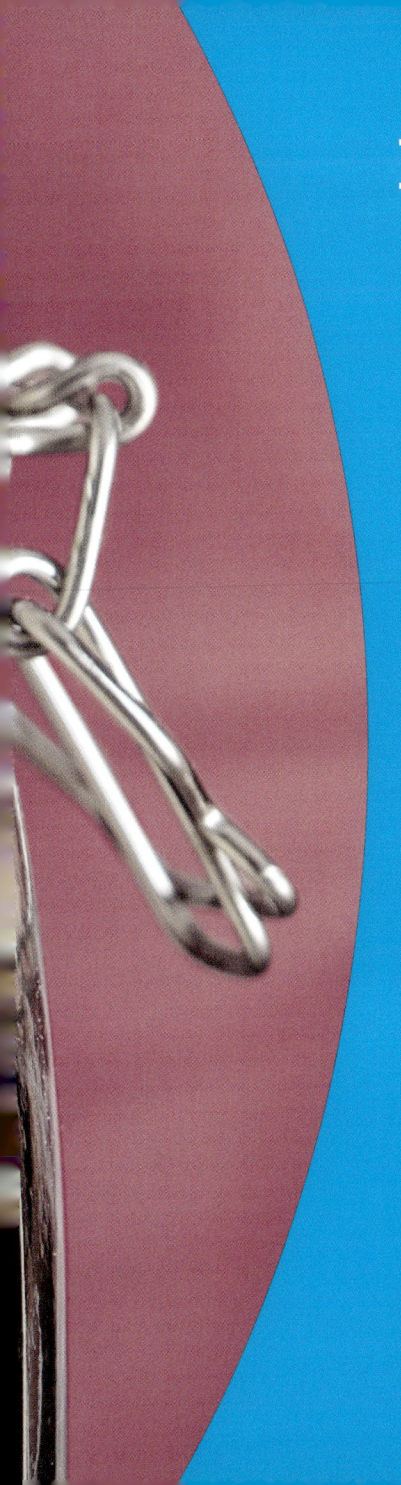

Flour has **volume**.
It takes up space.
All objects have volume.

The cookie jar is empty.

We make cookies!

Ingredients have volume.

ingredients

We can **measure** them.
We add flour.
How much?

Two cups (500 milliliters).

1 cup 250mL

1 cup 250mL

11

We add vanilla.

How much?

One teaspoon (5 mL).

vanilla

13

Ingredients fill the bowl.

We mix them.

The baking sheet is one foot (0.3 meters) wide.

It is two feet (0.6 m) long.

It fits 12 cookies.

There is one gallon (3.8 liters) of milk.

milk ·····▶

We pour a glass.

19

We fill the cookie jar.

Yum!

Measure Volume

Let's measure water to compare volume!

What You Need:
- two bowls that are the same size
- measuring cup
- measuring spoon
- water

Steps:
1. Measure one cup (250 mL) of water. Pour it into one of the bowls.
2. Measure one tablespoon (15 mL) of water. Pour it into the other bowl.

Which one has more volume? The cup or the tablespoon? How do you know?

Picture Glossary

gallon
A liquid measure equal to four quarts.

ingredients
Items used to make something.

measure
To find the size, weight, or amount of something.

volume
The amount of space something takes up within a container.

Index

baking sheet 16

bowl 15

cup 11

empty 4, 8

fill 5, 15, 20

flour 4, 7, 10

gallon 18

ingredients 8, 15

jar 4, 8, 20

measure 10

teaspoon 12

vanilla 12

To Learn More

Finding more information is as easy as 1, 2, 3.

❶ Go to **www.factsurfer.com**

❷ Enter "**volume**" into the search box.

❸ Choose your book to see a list of websites.

24